The Art of Living With Intent:

60 Days of Intentions and Inspirations to Transform Your Life

By Dr. Robert Kiltz

Copyright © 2011 by Dr. Robert Kiltz

All rights reserved. Except as permitted under the U.S. Copyright Act of 1976, no part of this publication may be reproduced, distributed, or transmitted in any form or by any means, or stored in a database or retrieval system, without the written permission of the publisher.

Published by Dr. Robert Kiltz
CNY Fertility Center
195 Intrepid Lane
Syracuse, NY 13205
www.cnyfertility.com

All rights reserved.

Published in the United States of America

ISBN: 978-0-9838458-6-7

First edition, Dr. Robert Kiltz, December 2011

For Mom and Dad, my teachers in life.

Introduction

Three years ago, I began something that has radically altered the very framework of my life. I started a practice that has forever changed me as a person.

Despite having a successful career, plenty of material things, a wonderful family, and great friends, there was something missing in my life. I was seeking happiness in all the wrong places. I worked too much, engaged in unsatisfying relationships, and constantly felt the loss of something I couldn't put my finger on.

Realize this: each and every one of us is constantly changing, whether intentionally or not. We are different people from who we were thirty years ago, two years ago, and even last week. Before I made a choice to change my life, I felt burdens upon me each day. The unhappiness was overwhelming. I refused to believe there was meaning to be found in my struggles.

Then I met two people who would profoundly change my life, Mark and Kristen Magnacca. This couple shared with me the simple technique of writing a daily, positive thought, an intention to create the day. This was an inspired notion from the Universe. It gradually became the guidance I longed for.

Nearly three years ago now, I began writing my daily intention. This is my practice of using my own words to express the beauty I feel inside and around me each day. Previously, I was unaware of how I allowed the television, weather, talk radio, and gossip to direct my life. These influences often put me in quite a fearful state of mind. The dreadful things I watched or read in the news often worried me. Anxious thoughts leaked into my subconscious through this exposure, and controlled my thoughts, distorting my perception of reality and leaving a cloud of insecurity ever looming, it seemed, over my head.

My daily intention encourages me to take control of how I feel and act. Each day, my positive, intentional thoughts lay the foundation for my success. I now understand what a drastic difference there is between an optimistic state of mind and a pessimistic one.

So I began using my daily intentions to motivate my staff, my clients, and others. But as much as I believed I was offering help to those people who were significant in both my business and personal life, I soon realized I was, in fact, on a journey to help myself.

Thinking is our nature. Through our thoughts, we create all things. Every thought we have creates a vibration in the universe. Our thoughts can manifest any number of experiential and material effects. A negative thought will attract negativity, a positive thought, positivity. This is the Law of Attraction, which has been described by innumerable sources since the dawn of time.

Our thoughts and attitudes in life are crucial. We can reverse our negative thought patterns and experiences simply by changing how we view our career, family, friends, and life as a whole. Start by appreciating the small stuff, like the hot cup of coffee you had this morning or a blue sky. We must allow ourselves to be open to love and positivity, and resist negative and emotionally unhealthy patterns of thought.

We must begin changing our lives by changing our thoughts and attitudes. It takes only 21 days to create a habit. Take the first step today and begin creating your own daily intention. Let this book assist you on your journey.

The Art of Living with Intent

1. Energy

"A strong, successful man is not the victim of his environment. He creates favorable conditions. His own inherent force and energy compel things to turn out as he desires."

—*Orison Swett Marden*

We are surrounded by abundant energy. It swirls around us as we float through life; sometimes unaware of the impact this energy has on us. Everything--from the sun, to the earth, to the trees--emits energy. It is this energy that binds us together as human beings. We are able to transfer this energy to our bodies, spirits and minds to create a spiritual manifestation within ourselves.

Think about the many energies that surround you, both physically and spiritually. Embrace these energies with your whole self, and feel the power within your body and mind. How does energy work to your advantage or disadvantage? Are you surrounded by positive energy? Do you allow negativity to create negative energy in your life? Think about how energy manifests itself in your life.

2. Dreaming

"Dream lofty dreams, and as you dream, so you shall become. Your vision is the promise of what you shall one day be; your ideal is the prophecy of what you shall at last unveil."

—James Allen

Our dreams are the manifestation of our hopes, fears, and subconscious thoughts communicating to us while we sleep. Our dreams hold the key to everything we desire and need to live our best, most inspired life. Sometimes our dreams can give us a sense of purpose and direction in life, and often, when we most need it.

Dreams also apply to our waking lives and prompt us to act based on knowledge or insight we have gained during sleep. Our higher self sends messages to us while we are sleeping that are for our highest good, secrets from the universe.

Even our aspirations and deepest desires appear in our dreams, and are sometimes even born from dreams. Realizations and epiphanies can occur when we are in touch with both our waking self and our subconscious thoughts.

The Art of Living with Intent

3. Selfless Love

"Transformation just happens when the selflessness of love blooms within the heart."

—Sri Swami Sai Premananda

Imagine yourself loving unconditionally your partner, your children, your family, your neighbors, your friends, and coworkers. Sharing your energy with them without any expectations of love coming back. Sending out positive rays of light and hope with loving gestures that project an aura of positivity around everyone you come into contact with.

Selfless love is when we love others regardless of their circumstances, behaviours, attitudes or beliefs. We love them without judgment or fear. We are able to see past the external things that don't matter and clear them away to make way for light and truth.

When you project selfless love, you are sharing a part of your being and teaching others how to selflessly love by inspiring them to do the same.

4. Life's Curves

"Every time you win, it diminishes the fear a little bit. You never really cancel the fear of losing; you keep challenging it."

—Arthur Ashe

The road of life has many curves. Sometimes these curves cause us tremendous fear. Fear that we might lose control, lose our way, or fail. What we often forget is that these curves are much less intimidating with the gift of sight. When we can look ahead and prepare for a curve it puts us in control of our own destiny. It allows us to take the wheel and hug the curves of the road closely with ease and perfection, even when the curve is steeper or trickier than we thought. The mere fact that we anticipate a curve helps us better maneuver.

Think of these curves as opportunities to grow and learn. Do not fear them or withdraw from the road, for these curves are what make life splendid. Love the curves. Hug the curves and embrace the light. Once you see the curves for what they really are, you will no longer feel at odds.

5. Thoughts

"We are what our thoughts have made us; so take care about what you think. Words are secondary. Thoughts live; they travel far."

—*Swami Vivekananda*

Our thoughts shape our reality. Everything begins with a single thought, be it negative or positive. When your energy shifts into thinking about something, you send vibrations out to the universe that attract the essence of those thoughts into your life. When you spend time thinking about something you really desire, you will attract and manifest that desire. Additionally, when you spend time thinking about something that you fear and do not want to happen or see, you are also attracting that into your life.

The specifics and details are unimportant here, as it is the essence and energy of your thoughts that create your reality. When you focus on finding happiness within yourself and stop seeking happiness in others, materials, and circumstances, you will attract abundant joy into your life. There are no limits, only limiting thoughts.

6. Everything's connected

"Nothing is accidental in the universe -- this is one of my Laws of Physics -- except the entire universe itself, which is Pure Accident, pure divinity."

—*Joyce Carol Oates*

Everything in our universe is connected and created from the same energy. Our thoughts become connected to the universe through the energy of our vibrations. The universe then responds to these vibrations by giving us what we need and guiding us on our intended path. Your feelings and emotions build the foundation of your thoughts, which are then brought into reality with action. Thoughts create action, so we must be mindful of our thoughts and understand how they are connected.

Once we come to terms with the wholeness of our universe and realize that we are all one, it becomes easier to see the messages from the universe that are there to help us navigate through life. When we follow our intended path, everything seems to come together beautifully and falls into place exactly as it should. When we are not following our intended path, things don't flow effortlessly and changes must be made. We can take our queue from the universe about where we need to change. We only need to listen to the knowledge we already have within us.

The Art of Living with Intent

7. Music & Spirituality

"Music washes away from the soul the dust of everyday life."

—Berthold Auerbach

Music has a deep connection with spirituality and allows us to feel peace, joy, inspired, reflective, and moved. When we connect with music it has the ability to give us a sense of belonging, and make us feel that everything is as it should be at that moment in time. We are able to connect with our spiritual selves through music and feel things that give us inner strength and connect us to the universe.

We will often feel divine when listening to music; the atmosphere and vibrational pulses around us deliver a tremendous sense of peace and connectedness. Music is universal in nature, and is really the language of our universe. Something we can all relate to and feel in our core. We all listen with our heart.

8. Openness

"Enjoying success requires the ability to adapt. Only by being open to change will you have a true opportunity to get the most from your talent."

—Nolan Ryan

Being open and allowing others into your heart isn't always an easy thing to do. We spend our lives building walls around us to protect us from getting hurt or feeling vulnerable, however these behaviors aren't really serving us well.

Our soul begins to feel harmonious when we allow it to share, love, and feel freely without fear of judgment or failure. Experiencing our environment with a sense of wonder and openness opens the door for possibility that would not have otherwise existed. We are suddenly able to create new opportunities for learning and experiencing our life and surroundings. Our open eyes and heart create excitement and great dialogue with others in our life. The opportunity to manifest real ideas also presents itself when our viewpoints are open and flexible.

9. The Writer within

"The art of writing is the art of discovering what you believe."

—David Hare

We all contain within us the sacred gift of creativity. The only difference being that some are more practiced with using their gift, and others more repressed. Writing is something that everyone can do regardless of skill, education, experience, and practice. You can begin to write today. Right now. And you will get better with time.

Writing has the ability to make you feel connected with yourself. Through writing you learn to understand yourself, and grow and evolve as a human being. Your thoughts deserve to be paid attention to. This is where writing comes in.

Believe that you are a creative being, that you have amazing thoughts and ideas and start the journey of discovering those thoughts through writing.

10. Inner Light

"Getting in touch with your true self must be your first priority."

—*Tom Hopkins*

We all contain within us an inner light that shines through our souls when we are living our best life and accepting the laws of the universe into our lives. All too often, however, the drudgery of day-to-day life takes over and we are unable to connect with that light. It leaves us feeling stressed out, dissatisfied, and sometimes depressed.

When we lose our inner light, it is because we are not concentrating on the source of true happiness, within ourselves. True happiness can only come from within and is not born from material wealth or from the relationships of those in our lives.

We begin to feel serene and happy when we are in tune with our inner light, and when we make time to connect with our spiritual selves. You take time out of your life to care for your loved ones; the same time must be taken to nurture your true self.

The Art of Living with Intent

11. Ask the Universe

"If water derives lucidity from stillness, how much more the faculties of the mind! The mind of the sage, being in repose, becomes the mirror of the universe, the speculum of all creation."

—*Chuang Tzu*

The universe has an order to it, and it too has a plan for us. When we need something to happen in our lives, or have a question we seek an answer to, the universe is there to provide us insight and help guide us. It is our job to learn to listen.

In our day-to-day lives, we are used to being resourceful to find the answers that we seek or to solve problems. We use technology, we rely on mentors, loved ones and experts, and we learn what we need to know in order to answer a question or solve a problem.

The same processes can and should be applied to our universe as it relates to our questions of life. The answers are already there and can be tapped into once we become aware of how to access them.

12. Individuality

"I am what is mine. Personality is the original personal property."

—Norman O. Brown

There is no better feeling than that of knowing yourself, loving yourself, and feeling free to express your individuality without fear. Embracing your individuality means being you even when the "you that you are" doesn't jive with what the rest of society may be doing.

You will know that you are being true to your individuality, because a sense of calmness, joy, and tranquility will come over you when you do the things that make you uniquely you. Embrace the quirks, love your oddities, be the unafraid you that is your true self. Be the unique and amazing you that inspires others.

Worry less about what things look like, what people think, or how others perceive you and focus more on what you think of yourself, and celebrate your individuality.

The Art of Living with Intent

The Art of Living with Intent

13. Left and Right Brain

"Your Design mind (right brain) attends to the melody of life, whereas your Sign mind (left brain) attends to the notes that compose the melodies. And here is the key to natural writing: the melodies must come first."

—*Gabriele Lusser Rico*

Most of us are inclined to rely more on either our left or our right brain. Our left brain is responsible for logic, process, and analytical thinking and controls the right side of our body. Our right brain is responsible for visual processing, creativity, and emotional intuitiveness. Our right brain controls the left side of our body.

Both sides of our brain are equally needed. We need our left side to help us understand and process our surroundings, keep us grounded, and bring order to our lives. We need the right side of our brain to help us dream, imagine, create, and think about "the big picture". Too often, however, we try to quiet our right brain, letting our left brain do the driving for us. We repress the intuitive flow of our artistic selves in favor of order and logic, when in fact the opposite would often serve us better.

14. Beautiful Day

"Looking for and enjoying beauty is a way to nourish the soul. The universe is in the habit of making beauty. There are flowers and songs, snowflakes and smiles, acts of great courage, laughter between friends, a job well done, the smell of fresh-baked bread. Beauty is everywhere."

—Matthew Fox

Often we wake up, brush our teeth, hurry out the door and go about our daily activities without being aware of the magic that surrounds us. We forget to breathe the fresh air into our lungs from our universe, smile at the sky and the clouds, feel the sun warm on our face, and truly marvel at the wonders of our surroundings. Everything we see, touch and feel comes from energy, everything around us once began as energy. It is important that we feel the energy from our environment and allow it to flow through our bodies. We are created from the same energy that the sky, soil, and water was born from.

When we become aware of our surroundings out in the world, we feel connected to our universe and a sense of "oneness" with nature. Using our senses to guide us, we begin to see the beauty in each day and look at the gifts nature has bestowed upon us with new eyes and appreciation. A tree that you see every single day may look completely different with this new awareness.

15. View from the Top

"Over every mountain there is a path, although it may not be seen from the valley."

—James Rogers

Imagine yourself climbing the highest mountain and standing on the peak surveying the valleys you have navigated below you. Life is all about altitude and attitude. Sometimes we are on top of the world, and other times we are down in the depths of despair. What we often forget is that without the journey to the top, we would have no means of appreciating being on the top. The view from the top just isn't the same without the hardship of the climb.

When we are on our intended path to the top, the universe responds with tranquility and harmony, however there are sometimes lessons to be learned on the journey to the top. We must take it in stride and remember that the view would be nothing without the valleys beneath us.

16. The Energy of Potential

"Human potential, though not always apparent, is there waiting to be discovered and invited forth."

—William W. Purkey

The potential we all have living and breathing inside of us creates abundant energy. The energy of things to come, things we desire, things we fear, and things that are within our grasp. It is up to us to tap into that energy and maximize the potential of our being. It is how we handle this energy that will determine the outcome.

There are many reasons why some of us are unable to tap into the energy of our own potential. Fear, motivation, and self esteem being three of the major factors. When we shift our thinking to disallow negative attitudes and thoughts into our consciousness, we are then able to allow ourselves the opportunity to reach our potential. Give yourself the opportunity to be who you are meant to be and revel in the joy of your potential. Know that you will get there by believing that you will.

17. Attitude is Everything

"Life is ten percent what happens to you and ninety percent how you respond to it."

—Lou Holtz

It's hard to not feel defeated, cynical, and negative sometimes. Lets face it, life is hard, and it gets us down sometimes. It's okay to let yourself feel a little melancholy at times, as long as you don't set up camp there and get comfortable. When you feel negative, know that it will pass. The hardship that you are experiencing is temporary. Things will improve. Know this.

Your attitude about yourself and your life will shape your reality. If you have a negative attitude, play the victim, or don't accept responsibility for things, you will find that life doesn't flow as smoothly as it could. However, when you accept that feelings are temporary and tell yourself that it will be okay, the universe will respond to those broadcasted feelings by making sure that it is okay.

18. Slow Down

"It's how we spend our time here and now, that really matters. If you are fed up with the way you have come to interact with time, change it."

—Wieder Marcia

We are all in such a hurry these days. Our lives are filled with hectic chaos, and we never seem to have enough time to slow down and breathe. Part of the problem is that we are never living in the moment, and are instead focused on the things we have to do, places we must go, or tasks we must accomplish. Never allowing ourselves to live in the moment means that we will never appreciate the best that life has to offer. We must allow ourselves to slow down and enjoy life in the moment. For that is where the magic of life lives.

Technology, while invented to save us time, also prevents us from enjoying the moment and speeds up time. We are constantly being interrupted by emails, phone calls, instant messages and information overload, especially when we are wired around the clock. Choosing to slow down means that we must be conscious about the things in life that prevent us from experiencing the moment, and work to limit the amount of time we dedicate to these things.

The Art of Living with Intent

19. Discover Your Artist

"All human beings are born with the same creative potential. Most people squander theirs away on a million superfluous things. I expend mine on one thing and one thing only: my art."

—Pablo Picasso

We all possess within us the gift of creativity, and whether you are conscious of it or not, an artist resides within you waiting for an opportunity to create and express. We all see beauty in the world, and an artist is simply one who transmits that beauty into something tangible like a painting, a sculpture, or a photograph. There are no rules about right and wrong with art, everything is right when you are creating.

It is easy to be lead by inspiration when you are an artist, but if you are not used to letting your creative energy lead you, it can be an intimidating thought. You may say to yourself "I am not an artist" or "I don't know how to create", but in reality you are an artist, you're just a little out of practice.

20. Soul Dance

"The dancer's body is simply the luminous manifestation of the soul."

—Isadora Duncan

Movement and music have a profound effect on our emotions. Music can move us to tears, reflection, joy, and excitement. Moving our bodies to the rhythm of the music reminds us of the soul body connection. Like music, dance is universal. It transcends age, gender, language, and religion. It is something we can all identify with, it has healing qualities to it that empower us and allow us to feel things we can only feel through dance.

Movement enhances our self-awareness, heightens our senses, and connects us to our surroundings. It is a powerful experience that we can use to get in touch with our soul and greater sense of purpose.

21. Words Heal

"It is chiefly through books that we enjoy the communion with superior minds. In the best books, authors talk to us, give us their most precious thoughts, and pour their souls into ours. God be thanked for books."

—William Ellery Channing

Sometimes we are unable to find the words or knowledge that we need to move from one cycle into another, or to shift our attitude to a more positive outlook. Books are often a source of comfort and healing and can provide us with the knowledge that we are unable to tap into within ourselves.

Reading a great book can be like finding a hidden treasure. A book can fill us with wonder, make us feel like we are a part of something larger, and allow us to heal ourselves through the soothing guidance of someone who helps us understand. Sometimes all it takes is holding up a mirror, and books can often be those mirrors that allow us to see what the universe wants us to see.

22. Messages from the Universe

"Once we make our decision, all things will come to us. Auspicious signs are not a superstition, but a confirmation. They are a response."

—Deng Ming-Dao

Throughout the duration of our lives, we are presented with gifts from the universe, which come to us in the form of signs. These signs exist to help guide us through life harmoniously and to let us know when we are living according to our intended paths or not. When we are living the life that we are meant to live, the universe tells us that we are on the right path by smiling on us and giving us a sense of peace, tranquility, and happiness. We know we are living well because we feel we are living well. Things just flow effortlessly, nothing feels forced or pushed and everything around us is in sync.

When we are not living according to our intended path, the universe responds to this by sending us messages. Things become hard, painful, or don't seem to work the way we so desperately want them to. When this happens, instead of asking yourself "why me?" ask yourself instead "what can I do to shift my thoughts and actions to produce a different outcome?" Once you become aware of these gifts from the universe, you will begin to recognize them more readily and will be able to apply them to your life.

The Art of Living with Intent

23. Discarding Thoughts

"A hundred wagon loads of thoughts will not pay a single ounce of debt."

—Italian Proverb

Thousands of thoughts go through our brains on a daily basis. It is truly staggering. Most of us aren't particularly aware of the thoughts we have and just let them happen without much acknowledgement. Some thoughts, however, are not helping us achieve our personal best and are instead limiting beliefs, which will hurt us rather than help us.

We must be mindful not to give too much power to negative thoughts and allow them to move through us, but not set up camp and stay for the long haul. Giving power to worry and negative thoughts will create a negative reality for us. Whatever we believe to be true becomes our reality.

Worries must be discarded. It is okay to acknowledge if we are afraid of something, however we must let the thought pass and not take us over.

24. Open your Heart

"I would rather have a mind opened by wonder than one closed by belief."

—Gerry Spence

Living with an open heart means opening yourself up to possibility, being kind and inclusive, loving your brothers and sisters of the universe, and being genuine and unafraid. This is not easy for many of us to do. We are often fearful of being hurt, rejected, judged, or appearing weak and vulnerable. So we build walls and wear masks that we can safely hide behind. We close ourselves to possibility by creating rules and logic in our minds that are safe for us, so we do not have to risk anything. This keeps us comfortable and lets us give as much as we are prepared to give, however, we are not giving our whole selves when we live in this light.

When we drop our guards and allow love into our hearts, we become free. Free from our own mental torment, and free to invite love and connection into our lives. Our relationships become deeper and stronger, our soul feels at peace, and we are able to see things that we didn't see before. It is worth the risk in every way.

25. Playful Spirit

"We do not stop playing because we grow old.

We grow old because we stop playing."

—Anonymous

    It's easy to deny ourselves, as adults, the sheer joy of play. We live in the fast lane and time is something that seems to be speeding up the older we get. So it isn't surprising that we don't think to nurture our inner child. Having a playful spirit does not mean regressing back to childhood, but it does mean having the openness, wonder, and adventurous spirit of a child by allowing yourself to explore, create, imagine, and play.

    Play is an extremely important part of the human experience and something that we simply cannot afford to overlook. It makes us feel alive, joyful, peaceful, and taps us into our higher intelligence. Our minds often lean too heavily on the left side, where rational thought and logic takeover. Play is largely associated with the right side of our brain, where creativity and imagination are the epicenter.

    Having a playful spirit will enrich your life in ways far beyond what you thought imaginable. Simply taking time out of our day to bring down our walls and adult rules, to be free-spirited and fun will open your eyes to human potential.

26. Our Inner Guide

"The soul's emphasis is always right."

—Ralph Waldo Emerson

We all have within us a spiritual guide that helps us navigate life by synchronizing with the universe. Our guide is there to heal us, help us, move us, and teach us. It tells us when we are off course, it gives us wisdom and messages about how to get back on course, and it is our spiritual barometer to determine where we are on our intended path in life. When we feel unhappy, hopeless or angry it is not because of any one particular event, it is bigger than that. It is because our spiritual self knows that we have veered away from our intended path and those emotions exist to help shine light on that. When we feel abundant, happy, fulfilled and at peace, it is because we are doing exactly what we should be doing. Living the way we are meant to live.

Our inner guide isn't always easy to listen to. It is always with us, but until we trust in it and allow it to guide us, we will have a difficult time. Our fears, expectations, and worries often impede our ability to hear the voice of our inner guide. Trust in your inner guide, know that it exists only to serve you and help you achieve your best life.

27. The Power of Visualization

"Visualize this thing that you want, see it, feel it, believe in it. Make your mental blue print, and begin to build."

—Robert Collier

You are the creator of your destiny. What you visualize, you create. How can you ever receive what you desire out of life if you cannot even see yourself having what you so desire? It is imperative that you learn to see yourself living in the light that you seek. See yourself experiencing the love of a soul mate, see yourself in the career of your dreams, see yourself with abundant wealth, and see yourself happy with all that you desire. It is not enough to simply want, we all want. You must align yourself with what you want by visualizing it and feeling with your very core that you will get there.

Once you are able to clearly see that which you desire, you are then able to move into vibrational alignment and allow these things into your life. Visualize your life the way you want it to be, smile and feel the warmth of that vision, and it will come to you. The universe will provide you with what you desire once you are able to see it clearly.

28. All is as it should be

"Everything is perfect in the universe -- even your desire to improve it."

—Wayne Dyer

Life becomes less stressful when we realize that everything we experience is self-created and exactly as it should be. We experience the joy, pain, sadness, and hardships in our life due to the thoughts we project. When we project joy and abundance, we attract joy and abundance. When we project pain and sadness, we attract pain and sadness. Everything in our life is a direct result of the vibrations we create with our thoughts. Everything we want and don't want comes to us if we spend our time thinking about those things.

When you know that all is as it should be, you can then begin to understand how to move out of a negative cycle and into a positive one. You are able to take back the power required to make the changes in your life that you so desperately want to see. Because it is all about you, and always has been. Nobody else has the power to create your reality. It is you and only you. All is as it should be.

29. Transformation is Within

"Keep constantly in mind in how many things you yourself have witnessed changes already. The universe is change, life is understanding."

—Marcus Aurelius

People are often aware that they need to make changes in their lives and will even go so far as to verbalize those changes, but they are unaware of how to truly make those changes. They are unaware that the transformation they seek must come from how they feel and not what they do. Transformation happens within, and when it does, the universe responds by changing circumstances around you and responding to the shift that has occurred within you.

Is your goal to be more patient, loving, or social? The only way that you will truly transform and allow these things to come to you is by practicing them. You must concentrate on your thoughts to ensure that they match the transformation you seek. Once you do that, you will invite this transformation to occur. You cannot change until both your thoughts and feelings change. That must be done first. You cannot change just your thoughts, and not your feelings, or just your feelings and not your thoughts. Both must be in tandem. Your emotional vibration has everything to do with what you manifest.

Know that transformation comes from within and is within all of our reach.

30. Our Mind's Movies

"Reprogramming the unconscious beliefs that block fuller awareness of creative/intuitive capabilities depends upon a key characteristic of the mind, namely that it responds to what is vividly imagined as though it were real experience."

—*Willis Harman*

We all have movies that play in our mind. Recurring thoughts, beliefs, fantasies, worries, and fears that keep us from manifesting the life that we desire. These ongoing movies are attracting exactly what we want or don't want by their mere presence. The more we play them, the stronger our energy becomes towards their manifestation. This is why it is extremely important to be mindful of the movies we play in our minds. Are they positive? Are they nurturing our spirit and helping us achieve the balance and success we seek in life?

It is possible to create our mind's movies to reflect a positive and inspirational outcome. We can condition ourselves to believe that the things we desire in life are within reach, and that we are working towards those things. All we essentially have to do is let each thought play out in our mind so that we create a vision of what we desire.

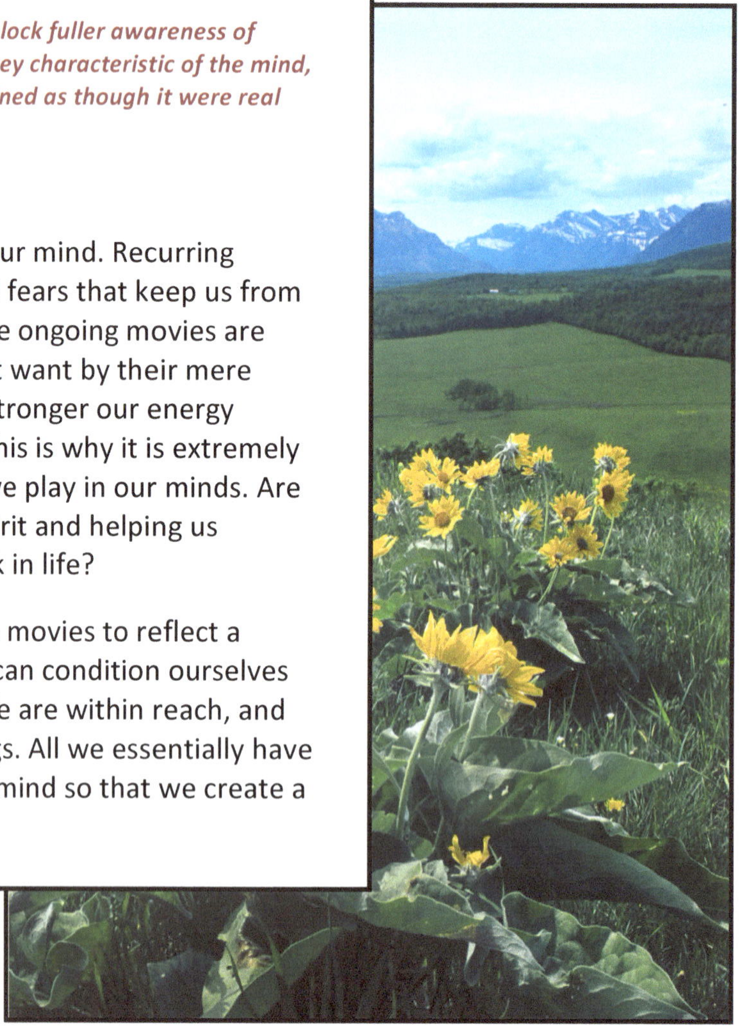

31. The Journey

"It is good to have an end to journey toward; but it is the journey that matters, in the end."

—*Ernest Hemingway*

We are often so concerned about what is going to happen next that we forget to enjoy the moment we are living in. We are rushed or too aware of time and lose sight of the magic of the universe and the very thing that shapes our future, this moment right now. The journey is more important than the destination, as life is a journey, and the journey is life. We must learn to see the joy in the journey.

Right at this moment you are on a journey through your own life. You are perpetually in motion, manifesting the things your energy attracts, and sending out vibrations to the universe based on how you feel. But are you forgetting to be mindful of the moment? Are you so focused on a destination that you are overlooking the journey? Never forget that this moment is what is paving the way for your future. Your thoughts, feelings, and energy make the journey all worthwhile. If you are too focused on a destination, you will never be able to enjoy the journey. Let each moment of your journey be filled with bliss, wonder, and contentment.

32. Embrace Change

"Observe constantly that all things take place by change, and accustom thyself to consider that the nature of the Universe loves nothing so much as to change the things which are, and to make new things like them."

—*Marcus Aurelius*

Our resistance to change is what makes our life hard. If we accepted change as part of the process and part of the experience, we wouldn't feel hurt, disappointed, or stressed when things change. We must adapt and expect change, because it is the one constant in life. Our universe is forever in motion, changing, expanding, breathing, and growing with our experiences and energy.

Embracing change is empowering and makes the journey of life much more enjoyable. When we are resistant to change, we are nurturing our fear. We are saying, "I can't handle not knowing what will happen, so I need things to stay the same." This is not how we evolve and grow as humans. Change is both necessary and beautiful. When we begin to embrace change and not fear the unknown, this allows us to be more open and experience true joy.

33. The First Step

"The journey of a thousand miles begins with one step."

—Lao Tzu

Progress cannot happen until one takes the first step. Anything we want to do, choose to do, or are thinking about doing must be followed by action. Simply wanting something will not make it so, but wanting something and then taking a small step towards that thing, will begin creating a momentum of energy towards manifesting that which we desire.

The magnitude of our goals really doesn't matter. The universe has no way of determining how large or small a goal is, and will only respond based on the vibrations that we put forth. If we are only thinking about something, but not doing anything about it, we will not be able to manifest that desire. But if we think about something, create a blue print for it, and then take a first step towards it, that is where we begin to see results. Our vibration will become strong enough for it to manifest.

It doesn't matter how small that first step may seem, it's the fact that it is taken that really matters.

34. Aligning with your Power

"If you are distressed by anything external, the pain is not due to the thing itself but to your own estimate of it; and this you have the power to revoke at any moment."

—Marcus Aurelius

Every human being on this planet is powerful. We all have within us the power of creation. It is one of the reasons we chose to be here in this body. The power to create is one of the divine characteristics of the universe. We have within us the ability to create our own destiny. The way that we create our destiny is by learning that our thoughts and energy create our reality. This is powerful knowledge to have, and once we have it in our arsenal, life flows in the direction we want it to go readily.

Aligning with our power simply means putting this knowledge into practice. We know that our thoughts create our reality, and that joy is the essence of experiencing the journey, so the real work comes in practicing this. We must be continually mindful of how we feel. Our hearts are significantly more intelligent than our minds, and are connected to the universe and it's energy.

35. Happy Home

"Home -- that blessed word, which opens to the human heart the most perfect glimpse of Heaven, and helps to carry it thither, as on an angel's wings."

—Lydia Maria Child

Home is for many of us our sanctuary, our escape from the drudgery of real life, and where our heart is filled with love. Our family, our pets, and our personal surroundings make us feel calm, centered, and at peace. Having a happy home is important to how we feel when we are out in the world. If things are chaotic, messy, unstable, or miserable at home, we will not be able to progress or feel confident in our day-to-day lives. Everything must begin at home, as this is where our day both begins and ends.

Our families are part of what makes home so wonderful. Having our loved ones around us makes us feel supported, loved, and confident that we can tackle whatever life throws our way. We must, however, ensure that we are taking time to enjoy the company of our loved ones, to tell them we love them, and to enjoy the moments we have with them. Too often the responsibility of life intrudes on our time with our family and takes us away from the moments that are joyous.

Having a happy home means embracing your family, enjoying time with them, feeling inspired by your surroundings, and enjoying the things you have. We must remember to be thankful for the people and things we have in our home, and cherish each moment.

36. Mindfulness

"On life's journey faith is nourishment, virtuous deeds are a shelter, wisdom is the light by day and right mindfulness is the protection by night. If a man lives a pure life, nothing can destroy him."

—Buddha

Mindfulness is one of the core teachings in the path to enlightenment. Being mindful means being aware of one's present moment and all of the senses, functions, and delights associated with that moment. It may sound simple, but it is not something that comes easily to most of us. Our brains are perpetually in motion causing us to think about things other than what we are doing in the present moment.

One of the simplest ways to begin being mindful is to be aware of our breathing. Slowing down, being comfortable and focusing on our breathing is a great way to bring us into the present moment. Being mindful brings a conscious awareness of the present. We can be mindful of the wind in the trees, the snowflakes falling from the sky, or the petals of a flower. It simply means we are recognizing the beauty in each moment, allowing ourselves to experience it wholly, without jumping into the future, as we tend to do.

Eventually when we are comfortable living in the moment, things that were once average or ordinary will become extraordinary and will be viewed in a whole new light. We will feel alive, present, and filled with joy.

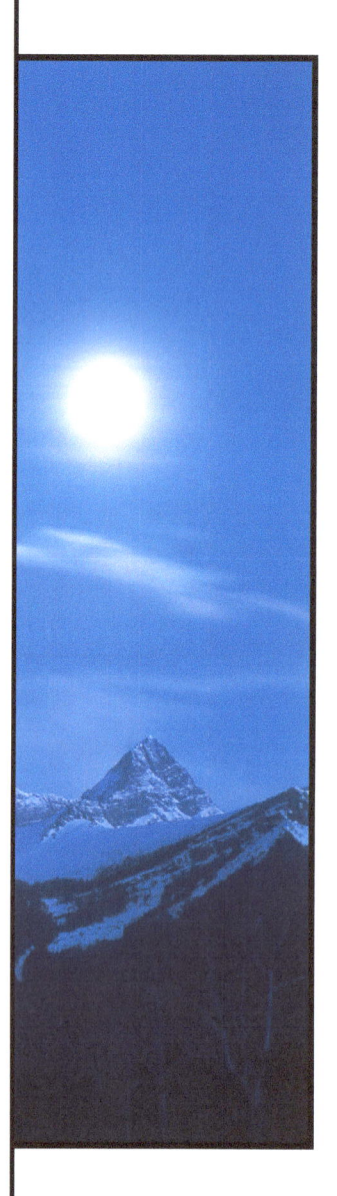

37. Creating You

"Be who you are and say what you feel, because those who mind don't matter, and those who matter don't mind."

—Dr. Suess

    You have the power of creation within you. The power to make yourself whoever you want to be, simply by visualizing and aligning your thoughts and behaviors with that visualization. This is something not to be taken lightly, for it is truly a gift that we continually have the ability to invent ourselves and become a direct manifestation of all that we desire. Life is not about finding ourselves, but about creating the person that we inside feel that we already are.

    When our inner being and our outer being is a vibrational match, we feel at peace with our surroundings and live an inspired life. We know that we are being our true selves, and we are solely responsible for that manifestation.

    We all have the tools within us to create the person we want to be. It is up to us to find and use the tools that are so readily available to us, and live the life that is intended for us. Creating ourselves is one of the greatest gifts of life, and success is when we become who we feel we were always meant to be.

38. Finding Energy

"Brain cells create ideas. Stress kills brain cells. Stress is not a good idea."

—Richard Saunders

When we feel unmotivated, down, or irritated, it is usually because we are disconnected with the universe. We feel uninspired by life and overwhelmed by the responsibilities and stress of it all. This is the first indicator that we need to find our energy and tap back into the universe to restore balance and peace to our lives.

Finding energy when you come from a place of stress and unbalance isn't always the easiest thing to do, but there are several things we can do to allow that energy to flow through our bodies, hearts and minds. First we must slow down and stop all of the stressful thoughts from invading our sense of calmness. It is these responsibilities, tasks, and problems that are causing us stress. Real life doesn't allow us to check out, but we can take a sanity break by slowing down and releasing ourselves of the pressure.

Remember, we are not here on this planet to make money, pay bills, and acquire material things. We are pure non-physical energy; our bodies just house us. When you need to tap back into that energy, think about the big picture. Why we're here, who we are, and what the purpose of life is. Think peaceful thoughts about love, connection, and universal oneness. For it is there, you will find the energy you seek.

39. Time

"A watch can only tell us how much time it is, how much time has passed, or how much time must still pass before something will occur. These statements are related not to time itself but only to its measurement or calculation."

—Medard Boss

The question of whether time actually exists, or whether it is a fictitious representation of measurement, is often discussed by physicists. As human beings, we constantly strive to control and understand our natural surroundings. Even though there are still many things in this universe that we have yet to understand. We cannot fathom the idea that time may not exist, because we are seemingly finite beings in an infinite universe.

Everything in our universe is in motion. Movement is everywhere and is the essence of life and energy. What if time had no beginning and no end, and was instead something that could not be measured? Our perception of time is our own doing and was created as a means to understand the universe. We cannot even describe what time is or speak to the qualities of it without referencing "time" itself. Where was time before man existed? How did we know that our perception of time (when we created it) was in sync with the true time of the universe? Think about how different our lives would be in the absence of time.

40. Pain & Suffering

"If you learn from your suffering, and really come to understand the lesson you were taught, you might be able to help someone else who's now in the phase you may have just completed. Maybe that's what it's all about after all."

—Anonymous

Pain & suffering is something that we as humans have all come into contact with throughout or lives. Even though our inner beings are pure joy and bliss, because we interact with the material world around us, we often experience the pain of change and rejection. We are most affected when things in our lives change drastically, making us feel out of sorts and disconnected with who we thought we were. This is evidence that we are feeling out of alignment with the universe.

It is hard for us to believe that pain & suffering is helping us in some way, especially when we are in the midst of it. But think of it as a gift and it may change your perception of how it should feel. The pain we experience in life is sometimes (not always) necessary for us to adapt to the changes that have occurred around us. We must transform from one state to another, which most often happens in the presence of change. Our pain is not a destination, but merely a stepping-stone on the road to joy. It is temporary and we will move through it triumphantly, coming out a better stronger person. Eventually when we see that pain & suffering is temporary, we will be able to limit its effect on our lives and allow pure divine love to take it's place.

41. Leading with your Heart

"Love is, above all, the gift of oneself."

—*Jean Anouilh Ardele*

Traditional Chinese medicine believes that the heart houses our consciousness and is connected to our emotions as well as our physical being. Our heart plays a big role in our emotional well being and our ability to have deep and meaningful relationships with others.

We were not put on this planet to protect our hearts from pain, to conceal our true loving nature in favor of indifference. Our emotions are the most intelligent part of our beings. Leading with our hearts is so essential to achieving human potential. We are here to love. Our inner beings are made up of pure divine love. To demonstrate anything else seems absurd and unnatural, but it is something that many of us do in order to protect ourselves. What we don't realize however is that in doing that; we are in fact doing the opposite. We are not protecting ourselves; we are hurting ourselves by being dishonest with who we really are. We are not allowing love into our lives and are creating an artificial reality. We are letting fear rule us instead of love.

When we lead with our hearts, and let love and happiness guide us, we are connecting with universal energy. We are inviting possibility into our lives, and we will discover that this is when inspiring things happen. Our soul will feel connected, and we will be in a position of allowing, rather than one of resistance.

42. Thoughts Become Things

"Watch your thoughts; they become words. Watch your words; they become actions. Watch your actions; they become habits. Watch your habits; they become character. Watch your character; it becomes your destiny."

—Anonymous

Each of us likely has an example of someone in our lives (perhaps even ourselves) that has lived out a self-fulfilling prophecy. When we consider how powerful our thoughts are, and how they lead us to act, it isn't surprising that negative thoughts beget negative reality. It is for this reason and this reason alone that we must be extremely mindful of the thoughts that we allow into our minds.

We all have undesirable thoughts from time to time, but it is when we build upon those undesirable thoughts and let the energy of those thoughts create an army of undesirable thoughts that we create problems for ourselves. We must always try to replace negative thoughts with positive ones. It is okay to acknowledge a negative thought, however, we then need to shift our energy to think about something more positive, or find a way to put a positive spin on it.

Thoughts become things, and the more thoughts there are about something, the more likely to manifest it is. Our minds are extremely powerful and can make or break us.

43. Ask & You Shall Receive

"Everything you want is out there waiting for you to ask. Everything you want also wants you. But you have to take action to get it."

—Jack Canfield

When we want something to happen we often spend our time on hope. We wish for things to be different, for things to happen for us, but we don't actually ask for what we desire. This is often the reason why our desires do not manifest. When we ask the universe for what we want, the energy of our asking creates the opportunity for our asking to transpire into something tangible.

We can ask the universe for guidance, answers, strength, or even something more specific that we would like to see happen. We must be careful, however, not to let doubt or fear factor into our mind when we are asking. We must believe in the power of the universe and have faith that our energy will manifest. If we do not believe, and simply ask for the sake of asking, manifestation cannot transpire. We must know in our core that real manifestation is possible, and that our prayers will be answered.

Sometimes the way in which the universe responds to our asking, may not be exactly what we were expecting. The result is the same, we have manifested our desire, but the route the universe takes to get us there may not be the same route we had imagined in our mind. We must be open to the various ways in which our desires may manifest.

44. Forgiveness

"Forgiveness is love in its most noble form."

—*Anonymous*

Because we are human, we are prone to bad judgment every once in a while. Sometimes people in our lives will wrong us and make us angry, upset, or hurt. This happens to all of us at one time or another. Sometimes we are on the receiving end of it, and other times we are the cause. The problem with these situations is that it exhausts our energy in a negative way. We spend time thinking about what "they" did to us, when in fact it is our inability to think constructively about the problem at hand that is the problem. If we change our thinking and handle it in a different manner, the outcome would be different.

We cannot control what other people do, nor should we try. We can only control our own interactions with life and our own thoughts and responses. This is precisely why the act of forgiveness is one of the most noble and loving things we can do. Forgiveness is a choice and it is very much an internal decision. We are choosing peace and emotional wellness when we choose forgiveness. To refuse forgiveness is choosing anger, resentment and emotional immaturity. When we deny forgiveness we are holding ourselves hostage to negativity.

Choosing forgiveness will allow us to move out of pain and into peace. It will add balance to our lives and create deeper relationships with others.

45. Stepping Stones

"One of the secrets of life is to make stepping stones out of stumbling blocks."

—Jack Penn

In life we are all faced with adversity and challenge. These situations are really stepping stones in disguise. Each and every problem, challenge or hardship we face is an opportunity for spiritual growth. These "problems" help us get to where we are going in life and allow us to connect with the infinite knowledge of the universe. Life is full of challenges; it is safe to say that challenge will be a continual presence in our life. This is precisely why we must learn to change the way we cope with challenge, and turn potential problems into opportunities by seeing the truth that lies within.

You will notice that people who seem to have good luck are the ones who have a positive outlook and embrace the notion that problems are opportunities in disguise. Alternatively, you will notice that people who experience bad luck are the ones who play the victim and get dragged down by their misfortune.

Without problems we wouldn't have the capacity to grow, learn and develop personally. We learn the most about ourselves while navigating these necessary stepping-stones.

46. Letting Go

"To design the future effectively, you must first let go of your past."

—Charles J. Givens

Attachment to desire is one of the primary reasons for human suffering. We easily attach ourselves to ideas, fantasies, expectations, and hopes. By attaching to those things, we are actually repelling what we want, instead of inviting it into our lives. It's okay to visualize desires, but we have to remain at a certain distance to those ideas. We have to feel grateful for who we are and what we have, and see those things as a joyful visualization, but nothing more.

When we let go of attachments, we close the door on suffering. Letting go doesn't mean throwing away or giving up. It simply means that we are happy with who we are and what we have at this very moment, and that we do not put all of our happiness into an external desire. It is very risky to hold onto attachments, and can cause us to feel emotionally bankrupt when something doesn't work out that we have put all of our hope and energy into thinking about.

Letting go enables us to tap into our inner strength and healing. The past will always hold us back if we continue to let it trap us. We must live in the present, let go of past pain and hurt, and let go of attachment. Only then will we tap into the harmonious and peaceful being that we truly are.

47. Personal Empowerment

"Don't let the negativity given to you by the world dis-empower you. Instead give to yourself that which empowers you."

—Les Brown

Attaining control and power over one's mind, body and soul is something many of us strive to achieve. Personal empowerment can help us in every aspect of life. It is when we tap into the wholeness that is us and feel empowered by our very being and potential. It is the knowing that we can be and do anything we desire. The knowing that we can achieve whatever we put our mind to, and the inherent knowledge that the universe will reward us with that which we desire when we are aligned with it.

There are a couple of important steps we must embark on to achieve personal empowerment. The first one is eliminating negative or limiting thoughts and beliefs. We must discard the thoughts that do not serve us and embrace the ones that will take us where we need to be. Action is the next step towards empowerment. We must take a small step towards the journey of our wholeness, whether this is taking a course, getting in shape, or getting in touch with our spirituality. The action that starts the momentum of our completeness will create the energy of personal empowerment.

48. Kind Heart

"A kind heart is a fountain of gladness making everything in its vicinity freshen into smiles."

—*Washington Irving*

Do you have a kind heart? Truly think about this question. Being kind-hearted is more than being nice or friendly. It is giving selflessly, acting with generosity and experiencing great joy in the happiness of others. Being kind-hearted does not necessarily mean being spiritual, and being spiritual does not always mean being kind-hearted. Being nice, unfortunately, does not always come from a kind heart. You must consider the motivations behind the behavior. When niceness comes from a kind heart, it is the embodiment of a spiritually enlightened being.

When you strip away fear, ego, and pride, you are able to invite joy into your life. Your heart can then be kind. And when your heart is kind, everything in your life becomes abundantly joyful. You will attract positive people, situations, and life lessons. Our true nature is to have a kind heart; it is only the impact of our human-built society that causes us to deviate from our true nature.

49. Life's Challenges

"Challenges are what make life interesting; overcoming them is what makes life meaningful."

—Joshua J. Marine

Any challenging event or circumstance in life that makes us feel uneasy, threatened, scared, sad, or angry is considered a challenge or a stressor. There are hundreds of stressors in our lives, and the degree of stress we feel towards a particular event depends on the individual personality. What stresses one person out, may not stress out another. We all, however, must deal with challenges in life.

The good news is that we can change our reality, so that challenges become opportunities for personal growth instead of paralyzing fearful events. When we are emotionally healthy, challenges don't bring us down or stop us from moving forward. We can successfully navigate life and learn from those opportunities. This is why focusing on our emotional health is imperative to living a happy, healthy life. Stress has many damaging effects on our minds and bodies. We must be aware of those effects, and make it a priority to manage stress effectively.

When we are emotionally intelligent enough to see challenges as opportunities, we evolve ourselves spiritually and can experience abundant joy.

50. Where are you Headed?

"The greatest discovery of my generation is that human beings can alter their lives by altering their attitudes of mind."

—William James

It's easy when we analyze our thoughts to predict the possible outcome of our future and to see where our energy is headed. When we are in control of our thoughts and are mindful about the type of thoughts we allow into our consciousness, we are better able to control the outcome of our life circumstances. When we let our thoughts control us and allow negativity, doubt, and fear into our consciousness, it manifests into our life by delivering a negative reality.

Our higher self does not make any distinction between positive and negative thoughts, harmful or helpful. We simply manifest the thoughts that we spend the most time and energy thinking about. This is the reason we must be mindful of our thoughts, because our thoughts tell us exactly where we are headed.

51. Energy Cannot Die

"We are not victims of aging, sickness and death. These are part of scenery, not the seer, who is immune to any form of change. This seer is the spirit, the expression of eternal being."

—Deepak Chopra

We are born from eternal energy. We come into these human bodies from energy that has not been created and therefore cannot be destroyed. Our energy is always here. Sometimes it is useful to think about this in relation to our lives here on earth. The energy of our being allows us to move through life, attracting things into our life based on the vibration of our energy. These vessels we call bodies house our source energy, which will never die. Our source energy is what makes us who we are and delivers to us the experiences in life that we seek out.

When you or someone you love dies, "they" have not really died. Their physical body has died. We are so much more than our physical bodies. We are made up of the same energy that creates everything in the universe and we are connected to everything. When we know this, it makes death easier to handle. Of course we always miss loved ones when they pass and will think about them frequently, but remember, they are still here. They always will be. Their energy still exists and is still in the air you breathe.

52. You Are the Creator

"There is no greater joy than that of feeling oneself a creator. The triumph of life is expressed by creation."

—Henri Bergson

Your life is a direct manifestation of your thoughts, fears and desires. It is a concept which many still have a hard time believing. It is difficult for some to fathom that God exists within all of us and that we are the creator of our own lives. Looking externally, outside ourselves for salvation, guidance, and direction takes our power away and enables us to be unaccountable for our lives. When we realize that the power resides within us and that we can control our own destiny by tapping into that power, life becomes a magical experience.

Know that you are the creator. This does not mean that you cannot still believe in God, religion, or follow a particular faith, but do not diminish the power that you have within yourself. Your being is much more than the skin, bone, and physical attributes you carry around with you. We are made up of pure energy; the same energy that all things are made from. You must believe in the vision you have for your life and be mindful of the energy you put forth. Have faith in knowing that you can have, and deserve to manifest the things in which you truly believe in. Make sure that your belief is pure, loving, and positive. It is this belief that will create the reality that you desire. You are the creator.

53. Child of the Universe

"If you must hold yourself up to your children as an object lesson, hold yourself up as a warning and not an example."

—George Bernard Shaw

Regardless of our physical age, we are all timeless children of the universe. Our soul dances with the energy of the universe and connects us to all that is. We are free to explore this universe with the same curiosity and wonder of a child, and this is exactly how we become connected and enlightened.

Unfortunately, as adults, we create divisions in humanity, constantly dividing ourselves by gender, race, religion, income, language, age, and social status. This divide is what prevents us from being able to experience the oneness that connects us all to the universe and everything in it.

A child lives in the moment and does not have any need for these human divides. In many ways, the younger and more pure our human selves are, the more spiritually enlightened we are. Our man-made environment takes us away from the universal oneness that is. It is up to us to realize that these divides are what hold us back. We must embrace the divinity and uniqueness of ourselves and learn to recognize it in everything else around us. Know that you are a child of the universe and feel the unity and oneness of that power, as you breathe in the energy of connectedness.

54. Dance with Life

"A thing of beauty is a joy for ever: Its loveliness increases; it will never pass into nothingness; but still will keep a bower quiet for us, and a sleep full of sweet dreams, and health, and quiet breathing."

—John Keats

If you knew that your purpose in life was to be happy, to experience joy and to live in the moment, you would dance with life graciously and without fear. You would feel the same enthusiasm you do dancing to your favorite song, feel the same rhythmic flow in your body and let each experience pass through you with loving intentions. This is exactly how life is meant to feel. Find the rhythm and move with the flow of your life. Don't fight it and go against the natural joy that you are supposed to feel.

Life is like a flowing river. It never stops, you cannot turn it in the other direction, you must jump into the river and dance with the swirling energy around you as it carries you downstream delightfully. Trust that the river of life will provide you with a magical dance. Let your feelings be your guide. If you feel good, you are in the river traveling downstream with a smile on your face. If you feel bad, you are trying to fight the direction of a rushing river and will never win. Dance with life, and let the universe be your favorite song.

55. Be Loving & Inclusive

"Give love and unconditional acceptance to those you encounter, and notice what happens."

—Wayne Dyer

One of the best things we can do to invite joyful abundance into our lives is to be loving & inclusive with everyone we come into contact with. It is easy to love the people in life who behave the way we want them to, or to love people who make our hearts swell. It is loving the people who irritate us, anger us, or who wrong us that is difficult. We must learn to forgive others and love them regardless of the place they come from. We can only control our own thoughts, actions, and behaviors, not anyone else's.

When we are loving & inclusive with all of our brothers and sisters of this planet, we invite joy and love back into our lives. We cannot experience pure love and joy when we come from a place of judgment, criticism, or anger. We must rise above that and choose to come from a place of love and forgiveness. We must consciously choose to love others and treat them with compassion and respect. And of course, above all else, we must love ourselves.

56. Being Happy / Happy Being

"Remember, happiness doesn't depend upon who you are or what you have, it depends solely upon what you think."

—Dale Carnegie

Choosing to be happy isn't always easy, especially when daily life and responsibilities drag our energy levels down and make us feel drained and defeated. We often forget the amazing magnitude of the universe in which we live. We go about our days without giving thought to the miracles that are occurring around us. We lead misguided lives and focus only on the unimportant things in life that do not resonate with our non-physical souls, and only serve our pesky left-brain.

Being happy should never be a destination. Don't look at it as somewhere you hope to arrive one day. Arrive there today. Right now. Instead of focusing on being happy, just be a happy being. You'll notice a profound effect on your mind, body and soul. Happiness is the most healing medicine of all. Live happy today.

57. Oneness

"Most of us experience happiness when we are enjoying life and feeling free, enjoying the process and products of our creative and intellectual processes, enjoying the ecstasy of transcendent oneness with the universe."

—James Muriel

Healing begins when we recognize that we are not separate from our universe, our brothers and sisters, the trees, the earth, and our atmosphere. We must break free from our minds and elevate our consciousness above our thoughts. Our beings are much more than our thoughts and come from a place of pure peace, joy, and enlightenment. We struggle and fight against things in life, which creates a divide within ourselves and turns our thoughts into negative self-harming weapons.

When we embrace Oneness, we accept that we are not our thoughts, that we are connected to everything in the universe, and we are able to feel inner peace. Attaining a state of Oneness will inspire others around you and will help them on their journey to enlightenment. Oneness is a feeling of interconnectedness and a separation from the human ego, which is essential to enlightenment.

58. Embracing Fun

"Live and work but do not forget to play, to have fun in life and really enjoy it."

—Eileen Caddy

We take our lives and ourselves too seriously sometimes. Life is supposed to be sheer joy, and if it isn't, then something is wrong. Are you inviting enough joy into your life? Things like work, finances, relationships, and family don't have to be stressful events if you train your mind to think about them in a different light. If something isn't fun or doesn't bring you joy, why are you doing it? You might think that is an overly simplistic viewpoint, but truly it is not. If there are things in life that are making you unhappy, STOP doing them… right now! If you hate your job, get a new one that you like. Is your relationship spiritually unfulfilling? It doesn't have to be. What about finances? Are you a worrier? Are you constantly playing catch up? The answer doesn't lie in more money; it lies in a change in attitude.

When you start embracing fun and seeking out joyful things in life that make you feel happy and satisfied, everything becomes lighter. Your eyes will smile, your heart will smile and your soul will smile. You will feel more gratitude for the things you have, and attract the things in life you want by not focusing on the fact that you don't have them. Your job is simple, find joy, embrace it, and have fun doing it!

59. Nothing is too far

"To accomplish great things, we must not only act, but also dream; not only plan, but also believe."

—Anatole France

Chances are if you believe that something is unrealistic or never going to happen, it will not manifest into your life. The reason it will not manifest has nothing to do with how possible it is, and everything to do with how possible you view it to be.

When you begin to view everything you've ever desired as being within your grasp, you suddenly realize that everything you've ever wanted is just a thought away. Nothing is too far, nothing too impossible or unrealistic. Everything is possible when you believe it to be. We must learn that the power of possibility lies within our being, not externally with circumstances or other people. We attract the things into our lives that we really believe in, the things that we spend our time thinking about, visualizing, and imagining.

Remember, everything you've ever wanted is possible. It all begins with the belief that it is possible. This belief must be genuine.

60. Carpe Diem

"Dreaming is wonderful, goal setting is crucial, but action is supreme. To make something great happen you must get busy and make it happen. Take that action step today that will put you on your path to achievement."

—Greg Werner

Today may be all that you have. All of us will die, but sadly, not all of us will truly live. One day our bodies will cease to support our human life, we will stop breathing, our hearts will stop beating and our energy will return to the universe. Each day of our lives is a gift, and we must appreciate every day we have here on earth. The only way we can appreciate and respect each day is to live in the present. We must learn to experience timelessness in a world that revolves around time and movement. We must stop, breathe, focus on what we are doing, and be present, for that is all that exists.

"Carpe Diem" (Seize the Day) means to enjoy life in the moment. Enjoy each second of the day. Live life to it's fullest in that moment. Use your senses to experience all that life has to offer and don't procrastinate. Now is the perfect time. No time is better than now. Forget about excuses like "I don't have time" and just do the things that bring joy to your life. The imposing of time restrictions is completely manufactured and does not have to apply to the present moment. Go outside and experience the joy that this universe has to offer each and every one of us. Happiness is yours. Take action.

Ingram Content Group UK Ltd.
Milton Keynes UK
UKHW050612240523
422181UK00002B/13